WITH

TRINITY BUSH

All Rights Reserved
Copyright © 2023
Beyond What You See, LLC

Produced, Published by
Legacy Brand Creators Publishing

No part of this book may be reproduced, stored in a retrieval system, or transmitted, in any form or by any means written, electronic, recording, or photocopying without the written permission of the creator Beyond What You See, LLC

Printed in the United States of America

First Printing, 2023

ISBN 978-1-7372752-7-5 Print
ISBN 978-1-7372752-6-8 eBook

Books may be purchased via www.BeyondWhatYouSee.net

TABLE OF CONTENTS

Foreword v

Introduction 1

Chapter 1: I Am Not Perfect, But I Am Enough 3

Chapter 2: How I Do It! 11

Chapter 3: Perfecting, Imperfect Me 17

Chapter 4: Self Care Is The Best Care 23

Chapter 5: Overcoming Adversity Using Positive Affirmations .. 31

Chapter 6: The Mental Rollercoaster 39

Chapter 7: The Pieces That Make Me, Me 43

Chapter 8: Breaking the Stigma 55

Chapter 9: Three Helping Hands 63

Chapter 10: The National American Miss Teen 69

Meet the Authors 79

Road to the Crown with Trinity Bush

FOREWORD
By: Patrice Bush

Raising a young queen, in an ever-changing culture and an ever-changing pageant world, has its challenges. Some of those challenges include the role social media plays in our girl's lives, the increased level of competition in our society generally, and this never-ending urge for youth to compare themselves to others.

Positive mental health has always been important to me because I understand the connection between our mental health and our everyday decision-making. As a professional counselor who is running a full-time private practice and the mom of the visionary author of this book, Miss Trinity, life is never short of opportunities to lean into my preteen and ensure her mental health is solid.

Trinity started participating in pageants at the age of 8. However, before I had allowed her to compete, I was completely against them because of their effects on mental health.

Pageants are commonly seen as a showcase of vanity and shallowness, and an additional life stressor. According to research from West Virginia University, they present a highly competitive atmosphere that could trigger comparisons, body disconformity, anxiety, and other mental disorders.

Four years later, I can say that some of these effects are true, some are not, and others can be managed with practice of good mental health.

As parents of pageant girls, it is important that we always keep their lives balanced. It is normal for adolescent girls to begin finding themselves, exploring and understanding their bodies, and becoming in tune with the emotions they may be feeling. And sometimes that normal development can cause anxiety. But when you add pageantry to an already stressful life stage, it can double the struggle. So helping them understand what's normal and when they might need to seek help is important.

In our household, we always ensure that each of us are aware of our feelings and support each other when we need help processing or managing them. In pageantry, I always remind Trinity of her purpose. I always remind her that what is INSIDE her is what earns her the crown, not what is outside. This aids in ensuring that her mental health is always in good condition.

Here are a few of my tried-and-true methods to help Trinity maintain good mental health:

1. Help her to see herself as queen whether she wins the crown or not.

2. Make sure to compliment her frequently. I focus more on internal compliments that feed her soul, not just her appearance.

3. Let her know it's okay to feel any emotion. We can't hurt others with our emotions, but we can feel them and own them.

4. Explain what therapy is and always remind her that it's a resource readily available to her when she needs it.

5. Never make statements about her body, weight, or size that could damage her self-esteem.

6. Trinity created audio affirmations during the pandemic. I ensure that she doesn't just share those with others but also says them to herself regularly.

7. Lastly, we review the results from her pageants with a non-critical eye that acknowledges all that she did well and continues to learn the industry.

Every parent has a major role in helping their children maintain a positive mental health. We have life experiences that have taught us what happens when we don't, so it's important that we walk beside our children and lay the foundation. But you don't have to take my word for this. Instead, these inspiring stories about ten wonderful Queens will help you understand the connection between pageantry and mental health.

Road to the Crown with Trinity Bush

INTRODUCTION

If there is one thing that I will tell the 4-year-old pageant queen, Cayeton, it is that you are still on the road to the crown.

Growing up in the pageant world as a dark-skinned beautiful little girl, I knew I had one job: TAKE THE CROWN HOME! I knew, when it was my time to walk on stage in my fun fashion outfit, that I needed to set the floor on fire! And it was exactly what I was supposed to do because I left the pageant weekend with a winner's title!

Every few months, I competed for something that I enjoyed doing. However, it did become mentally draining. Now that I am older, I understood why I felt tired and overworked. As a child, even if I voiced my discomforts, I would be told to repeat the routine until I got it right. I only had so little time to take naps during breaks as the girls were competing on stage. I also couldn't eat heavy meals because I was told that it would make me look bloated (Oh, I was so hungry!). I wore beautiful dresses and costume pieces that made me feel uncomfortable at times even if I looked good. But I had to listen to my mom because I didn't want to make her upset.

In 2023, the pageant world is still booming, but a lot has changed. They have become more diverse, and the competition is much tougher. Girls of all ages that come from everywhere compete for one title, once a year. The buildup to the pageant weekend becomes stressful, not only to the moms, but even to the girls who are worried about defeating the competition and winning the crown. As fun as pageantry can be, so much happens behind the scenes that it becomes taxing to the girls mentally, emotionally, and physically.

As such, mental health in the pageant world is extremely important! As girls, we think of so much at one time, and it can be unhealthy. As queens, we have to protect our mind by making a difference and changing the dynamics to positive pageantry.

Each author in this book reveals that pageantry has its downfalls. The queens had the amazing opportunity to identify these issues, and now they are on the road to becoming queens who are ready to make a difference in our world, in what we have passions for, and in the pageant world!

Here is a message to the queen who reads this book:

> A crown and a sash do not make you a queen. What makes you a queen is your ability to see other people and make a difference in their lives. You are royalty, and nothing can change that.

Plan. Passion. Action!

~ **Cayeton J. Norton,**
Miss Mission USA Georgia 2023

Chapter 1
I AM NOT PERFECT, BUT I AM ENOUGH
TRINITY BUSH

There is no greater agony than bearing an untold story inside you.
~ Maya Angelou

I am more than I think I am

Other people's opinions do not define me

Courage is my superpower

Even when I'm scared, I'll do it anyway

Hello! My name is Trinity Bush, and I am the CEO and founder of Beyond What You See. I am an author, pageant queen, business owner, affirmation slanger, and certified public speaker. At Beyond What You See, I help kids build self-confidence and self-esteem through my audio affirmations, affirmation t-shirts, fashion shows, and my books. My business is inspired by the definition of mental health, and my services teach how to help maintain a healthy mind.

> Mental health: a person's condition with regard to their psychological and emotional well-being.

> Self-care: the practice of taking action to preserve or improve one's own health.

What does mental health mean to you? What does self-care mean to you?

Having positive mental health is important to our development as kids and teens. Most of us are talking about our feelings, but we don't know that our emotions are connected to our mental health. Our mental health affects how we think, feel, and act, and determines how we handle stress and make choices.

You know what I noticed? I noticed that not all kids are as confident as I am. I had no idea that there are kids in the world who actually feel bad about themselves, so much so that it affects the way they learn, behave, and experience life!

Do you know any bullies or people who pick on others? People who don't feel good about themselves tend to put others down. It's a vicious cycle, and it's one way we can tell if someone's mental health is not stable. If you are bullying or picking on others, your mental health is not strong. Mentally strong kids are not bullies. They are aware of the things they say or do so they won't hurt someone else. They make decisions that show they care about themselves and other people.

While I have never been bullied myself, I have been talked about. Kids in my class at school would make comments like, "OMG, Trinity you're so small." I know I'm smaller than them. They didn't have to tell ME! I didn't like it. It made me feel less than. But I remember my mom always reminding me that I am not perfect, but I am enough. That statement got me those ugly comments by my classmates.

Did you know that you are more likely to succeed in life if you have self-love and self-confidence? It is important for everyone to prioritize these two so they will know their worth. 75% of girls with low self-esteem have reported engaging in negative activities like cutting, bullying, smoking, and eating disorders. Meanwhile, over 70% of girls avoid daily activities such as attending school when they feel bad about their looks. This is a real issue!

We can't leave boys out of the conversation as well. 30% of middle school boys report having low self-esteem due to increased pressure to pursue an intimate partner, perform well athletically, and focus on physical image.

Did you also know that insecure kids grow up to be self-conscious adults? Being self-conscious can grow with you. If you never stop a bad habit, it will never go away. And it will affect your life in the future and how you accomplish things. We gotta remember that we are not perfect, but we are enough.

My mission is to make a WORLDWIDE IMPACT by helping others with confidence. And I want to share some steps with you to help you take care of your mental health too!

1. Share how you feel whenever necessary. You can tell a friend that they hurt your feelings by something they said or tell them how grateful you are to have them in your life. For example, one of my friends said something I didn't like and I had to tell them how I felt about what they said. My expression of my feelings helped me to feel better and not take what they said personally. My mom always says that expressing your feelings is therapeutic.

2. Finding and joining social groups, sports teams, and being around friends that make you feel good and accepted. I get along with everyone. Being around people can be fun. During my state pageant, I was really nervous because I looked different from my other peers. Everyone else was much taller than me, and I wasn't sure I would fit in and that I would be accepted in the group of junior preteens. To my surprise, we all got along great and became friends due to our commonality of pageantry!

3. Create a self-care routine. This one is my favorite! Something that I do that makes me feel better when I'm

stressed, worried, or just need a break is self-care. I love getting pedicures, manicures, and going shopping. I take nice long showers too. After that, I do skincare. I do this because taking care of myself makes me feel good, happy, and relaxed.

4. Focus on learning to enjoy every moment. If I feel like dancing, I dance. When I'm happy, I sing, and I don't care who is around! When I am in pageant mode, I am in my happy place. Even though it's a competition, I live every moment. I embrace every opportunity to smile, laugh, dance, and just enjoy myself.

5. Lastly, get out and engage in physical activities. Moving around and playing with others helps increase endorphins. Endorphins are chemicals in our brain that help us feel good! One of my favorite things to do is jump on my trampoline. I also developed a new love this school year, and that is basketball. Even though I am new to the sport, all of the running and physical aspects make me happy and help me to feel good on the inside.

So I want you to think of something that you enjoy doing or things that make you feel good. Write them down. Now I want you to pay attention to what those things are and what they have in common. Now I want you to think of things that worry you or stress you out. Write those down too. Then look at those and pay attention to how they make you feel. Do they make you feel overwhelmed or like you have no control? Like you're losing yourself? If they make you feel something like any of those 3, they are not something to have in your life.

Mental health is very important, and it is something you should begin thinking about even now. What are you going to do to maintain it? Will you join a group at school? Will you find someone to talk to? Or will you create a self-care routine? Whatever you do, start today. It will be the greatest gift you could give to yourself.

I have something I want you to say out loud. It is the title of this chapter and the sentence you have read many times here. You ready? Let's go!

I am not perfect, but I am enough! I am not perfect, but I am enough.

I Am Not Perfect, But I Am Enough

Personal Reflections

Road to the Crown with Trinity Bush

Chapter 2
HOW I DO IT!
SELENE M.K FERDINAND

Love yourself every day, and be the sunshine on every cloudy day even if the sky is dark.
~ Selene Ferdinand

An apple a day might keep the doctor away! But for me, having berries everyday keeps my mental health on the right path!

I love sour berries, sweet berries, and I love berries in my pancakes. I love berries in my smoothies, in my salad, in my desserts. I love to start my day with a slice of whole wheat bread and my homemade berry jam.

Being a public speaker and a pageant queen, it might not seem stressful for a 10-year-old. But mental health helps determine how we handle stress, relate to others, and make healthy choices. And good mental health is important at every stage of life, from childhood and adolescence to adulthood, because it includes our emotional, psychological, and social well-being. It affects how we think, feel, and act.

Pageants play a huge role with my mental health. They always remind me that I don't have to be beautiful to fit into the world. With my self-confidence, I can move any mountain! They also make me feel extremely excited, comfortable, and confident when I am on stage. However, the backstage is where all the stress takes place, especially when a stranger has to escort you into the stage.

My first year was the most awful! We went on one of the NAM open calls where one of the staff members advised the parents, "It's better for someone else to escort your child because sometimes they hold on to a family member." My Mom took the advice and had someone else to escort me on stage. Uh oh! It didn't work. I refused. I put my feet down and I said I'm not going to do it.

So my brother Stefan said he was going to escort me. Since then, he has been my escort. With my brother by my side, it makes a big difference in my confidence and my lack of communication skills; family is the number one remedy to treat your mental health.

There's also my auntie Rachelle who would always say to me, "Selene, when you are stressed, just close your eyes and sing your favorite song in your head." Guess what? It works!

Being a pageant queen and living in a non-pageant world is not easy. But with the confidence of the Almighty Lord, my family, and my personal friends, I can walk with my head up in the sky and my feet firmly on the ground. I feel that I can take on the world.

So my friend, your family and friends should be the first people you trust in your life whom you should speak to about your mental health. But when I said family, it does not have to be your blood relative. You might have a better relationship with your next-door neighbor. If you are having a mental breakdown, seek help! Always remember that the people you spend time with in your everyday life cares for you! Speak to them if something bothers you.

Whenever I feel down, I sing, dance, listen to music, or help Mom in the garden. Playing with dirt relaxes me while music helps my mental health; by listening to music that uplifts, empowers, and inspires me, I feel powerful and outgoing. And since music is a type of art, I may just tell you about my love for arts and crafts.

Art is one of my favorite subjects. It's not only fun, but also calming for me. I love painting portraits of flowers because it adds texture, though sometimes the paintings can come out a little bumpy or rough like the emotional and sad times in life. But the paintings could also be smooth like the good and exciting times.

To help me with the rough times, I meditate by sitting criss-cross applesauce in a comfortable and quiet place, then I would hold a flower. Each petal represents a hard time or a time I had a strong feeling about myself, so I imagine being surrounded by my favorite flower...

I love to snack on sour berries when I am stressed. It helps me relax and think positively, and it is good for the brain. There are compounds, found almost exclusively in berries, that help in learning and memory, thus maintaining good mental health. You should try berries when you feel overwhelmed.

Besides berries, the things I wear in pageants and I do for my community also help improve my mental health. When I run out of berries, I love to put on my favorite high-heeled shoes and fancy dresses, and then I sprint around the house, dancing my way throughout my community with my non-profit organization Meera Empowerment, empowering the youth of tomorrow with my fun fashion shows, tea parties, arts and crafts, cooking classes with my Mom, and cooking at Ronald McDonald House to promote mental health.

Having fun and lots of laughter remind me how less stressful life can be. That's why I co-host on You're Our Unity with Mrs. Lashawn Walker on Strong Island Television, not only to empower the youth in my community about mental health, but also the whole country. I might seem only 10 years old, but this 10-year-old has the mind of a 30-year-old. I feel empowered when an adult sit and listen to what I have to say. By having an adult listen to me, it energizes me to become a more active person.

I want to grow my self-confidence! I am a very confident and outgoing person. However, sometimes I still get butterflies in my stomach.

Mental health is an essential aspect of overall well-being and should be given the same attention and care as physical health. It's estimated that 970 million people worldwide have a mental health or substance use disorder.

So eat healthy and enjoy mother nature, my friends. Stay active and always remember that the sky's the limit. As my Mom always says: "Turn your can't into cans and your dreams into plans."

Five things that can improve your mental health:

1. Focus on the present and appreciate the little things in life.
2. Do things that make you excited and happy, like dancing or singing.
3. Exercise regularly.
4. Practice stress relievers such as meditation and yoga.
5. Eat a healthy and balanced diet.

Personal Reflections

Chapter 3
PERFECTING, IMPERFECT ME
ZARIA MARTIN RILEY

> *Depression doesn't take away your talents-*
> *it makes them harder to find.*
> *~ Lady Gaga*

I always dreamed of being the perfect model and winning pageantry titles. But as I stepped into the world of pageants, I faced challenges that shook my belief in myself. In my first year, I didn't win anything, and it made me doubt myself. It hurt even more when others copied me and won everything. I felt like a failure, and it was tough.

As I grew older, my body started changing, and it became hard to find dresses that fit. I gained weight, and my self-esteem went down even more. I used to think finding pretty dresses would be easy, but as I grew bigger, it got harder. My brothers and kids at school teased me, and I felt like pageantry wasn't for me anymore.

But I didn't give up. I turned to modeling instead. At first, things went well, but then my self-esteem took a nosedive again, even lower than before. I struggled with depression, and it got worse each day. Peer pressure got to me, especially on social media. I tried to be like everyone else so I wouldn't be left behind. It was a tough year, but my mom got me a therapist to talk to.

In 2022, I didn't love myself as much. I wore hoodies and leggings to hide. I felt alone most of the time, and my parents didn't seem to understand how I felt. I hung out with the wrong people, and they weren't really my friends. They would only be nice when it suited them. It hurt when they promised to play with me but then said they couldn't. I often ended up sitting alone at the lunch table or working by myself. I wondered if anyone truly liked me.

Despite everything, I still got straight A's in school. Talking to my therapist made me realize that I didn't need people by my side to be great. The only person I truly needed was myself. My body going through puberty caused some behavioral issues, like talking back to my mom. But I was trying my best to change and improve.

I had to learn how to respond to things. Sometimes, my emotions would get out of control, even over small things. It felt like shaking a soda bottle and then opening it. But I knew I had to keep trying.

As the end of 2022 approached, I started making goals for the next year. One of them was to take care of myself and put myself first. Then suddenly, 2023 arrived. The first weeks were okay, but then everything went wrong. I started feeling down and alone again. I thought it would be an amazing year, but it didn't go as planned. And then my birthday came on January 31st. It seemed like nobody remembered, except for my family. It made me really sad because I thought others would remember too.

During those tough times, I turned to journaling. I would write in my journal about how I felt ugly and how I hated my life. I was hurting so much that I couldn't control my feelings anymore. Sometimes, I wished I wasn't alive. But my therapist helped me realize that deep down, I wanted to live. I just wanted the pain to stop. Writing in my journal helped me release those emotions and thoughts.

Journaling and writing became my way of venting to myself. When I felt lonely or struggled with confidence and self-love, I would write in my journal. Sometimes, I didn't want to talk to others about what I was going through, and it felt like nobody was there for me. So, I turned to my journal as a safe space.

If you want to try journaling too, I have some advice for you. Always keep a notebook and pen with you wherever you go. You never know when you might have a bad day or experience something scary or embarrassing. When those moments happen, you can spend 5 to 10 minutes writing about it in your journal. You can also write daily affirmations or say them in front of a mirror to boost your confidence.

The most important lesson I learned through my journaling journey is to never stop loving yourself. Even though I went through tough times, I discovered how to maintain self-love. Whenever I feel down or overwhelmed, I turn to my journal and write. It helps me express my feelings and understand myself better.

Now, it's your turn to write. How did my story resonate with you? How can you use journaling to help you on your own journey?

Grab a pen, open your journal, and let your thoughts and emotions flow onto the pages.

Remember, you are not alone, and your story matters. Embrace the power of journaling and let it guide you to a place of self-love, healing, and growth.

Perfecting, Imperfect Me

Personal Reflections

Road to the Crown with Trinity Bush

Chapter 4
SELF CARE IS THE BEST CARE
JAZEL BELLA JOHNSON

Love life. Engage in it. Give it all you've got.
Love it with a passion because life truly does give back,
many times over, what you put into it.
~ Maya Angelou

I always carry with me a simple yet profound reminder: self-care is the best care. It reminds me of the instructions given by flight attendants during safety protocols. They instruct us that, in the event of an emergency, we should secure our own oxygen masks first before assisting others. This resonates deeply with me because it reinforces the idea that we can't truly help others if we haven't taken care of ourselves first.

Mental health is a powerful force that impacts every aspect of our lives—our thoughts, actions, words, and self-expression. In today's society, it has rightfully taken center stage as an important topic. Remember that everyone experiences their own struggles, and it may be challenging for them to express what they're going through. That's why, before reaching out to help others, it's important to prioritize your own self-care.

This is my story. Pageants take a lot of work and time. If you want to win, you need to be trained and ready for anything that comes.

During my second pageant, I had encountered one of the most challenging experiences of my life. I was in the backstage waiting to do my personal introduction. There were at least 15 to 20 girls in front of me. They all have been doing pageants their whole life, and they were all prepared and just relaxing. But there I was panicking and wiping the sweat off my head. My heart was bumping out of my chest. I felt like an amateur because everyone was calm and collective. It felt like I had five billion eyes all over my body and everyone was looking at me. While I was panicking, I forgot my entire speech. I thought to myself, Jazel, you can do this!!!

At that point, there were still at least 10 girls in front of me. I tried to put some of the main ideas and words together, but they didn't make any sense. All I could think about was my positive affirmations and using them as my strength. Then we were lining up and there were just about 4 girls in front of me. This was not my first time doing this. I am used to being in the spotlight and having to memorize things and recite it. For example, when I led the countdown and performed at the Holiday Tree Light Show for my city or when I had to memorize the lines for my school musical.

I was trying to calm down. Why am I acting like this? Something was not right, but I could not put my finger on it. My thoughts were scrambled, and I was thinking about everything but my speech.

Soon I heard them call my number, and I knew it was showtime. I was nervous and trying hard to stay focused. My nerves had gotten the best of me. You know when people say they feel butterflies in their stomach when they are nervous? I felt heavy bricks in mine at the time.

But something caught my attention. I looked up across the room and saw the table full of awards, and my eyes connected with the first place awards. And then I was able to collect myself and regain focus. I remember the reason why I was here, and that was to win. I prayed to God for his help and guidance, now and always.

I remember what I do when I get nervous about something. It was to think of something that I love and say some affirmations. I thought of this one time when my family and I went to South Carolina for Thanksgiving. I visited all my family and went to the beach and pool. It was one of the best times I've ever had. That calmed me down, but I still wasn't completely myself. So I closed my eyes and said, "You are beautiful, smart, hardworking, strong, and talented." By the time I opened my eyes, I had to go on stage. I took one breath in and out, and everything came back naturally. My prayer was answered.

By doing this technique, everything went as smooth as could be. I did not just do my personal introduction; I nailed it. I made eye contact with all of the judges and smiled. My confidence was out of this world. I stood there with happiness and warmth in my heart. You would never think what happened backstage was still going on. I felt so in the moment and felt so much better. I was glued to the stage and did not want to leave. Even though it was a competition, I felt like tons of stress had left my body.

While walking away, I felt amazing, like I could conquer anything. After everyone went, we were dismissed to the hall. I had to get ready for my next event. I did my hair and put on my outfit for our interviews. That was my most favorite event, including optionals. I took my break, then it was time for me to refocus and get my head back in the game.

After all of the events were completed, it was finally time for the award ceremony. Before I went onto the stage, my family and I said a prayer. Then all of the girls lined up, and it was time.

In the last 5 minutes, I repeated my affirmations: "You are beautiful, smart, hardworking, strong, and talented." I walked up to the stage with the best smile ever and was just so happy that I was given this opportunity.

While I was at the award ceremony, I never heard anyone call my name so many times before. Every five seconds, my name was being called for an award. I was in the middle row, so it took me some time to walk back and forth every five seconds. All I could think about was how it was all so worth it. I remember taking so many pictures until my smile was almost permanent. It was a really amazing time that I will always hold dear to my heart. I won multiple awards in numerous different categories.

Throughout my journey, I've discovered some incredible lessons that have transformed my life. I want to share these uplifting experiences with my readers, especially the little girls who may be facing their own challenges. One thing I've learned is that the power of proper breathing and positive thoughts is truly remarkable. It may take time, but with patience as our guide, we unlock the doors to wisdom and growth.

Most importantly, I want every reader to know that they are never alone. My own experiences in pageantry have left a profound impact on my life, and I've learned valuable techniques along the way. Despite the occasional hurdles we encounter, the outcome is always worth it.

Positive affirmations have become my guiding light, lifting my spirits and allowing me to embrace my true self. Through focused breathing techniques, I find calmness and clarity, gathering my thoughts with ease. Embracing positive thoughts has opened my eyes to the realization that everything happens for a purpose. With these tools, I feel a newfound sense of openness, positivity, and freedom from stress.

Learning these techniques are pretty simple and rather easy to implement in your everyday life. While thinking of something happy, you have to be in the right mindset to do so. What I mean by that is that you should try to calm yourself down first. When you are not at ease or feeling stressful, these techniques work. The first thing I do is close my eyes for 5 seconds and think of something that makes me smile. While doing that, you should only think about doing happy things that put a smile on your face. After that, what I like to do is some breathing techniques. I breathe in and out a couple times, but you have to do them slowly. Lastly, I say my positive affirmations. My affirmations are something I say daily, especially when I first wake up. By doing these, everything becomes easier and I am ready to conquer the world.

Mental health is something that should always be at the forefront of all that you say, do, and think. One must protect their mental health as well as others around them. One of the keys to this is by being kind to yourself and others. I encourage everyone to check in with yourself to make sure you are self-aware of anything that may be challenging you or having an effect on you. Never be afraid to address the state of your mental health and to get help if you ever need it. There is only one you on this Earth, and each day your goal should be to continue being a better version of yourself. Always remember to Breathe, Pray, Relax, and Go Forth.

Self Care Is The Best Care

Personal Reflections

Road to the Crown with Trinity Bush

Chapter 5
OVERCOMING ADVERSITY USING POSITIVE AFFIRMATIONS
DARIYA LARRY

*She is clothed with strength and dignity,
and she laughs without fear of the future.*
~ Proverbs 31:25

Boom, boom… Boom, boom… Boom, boom. The rhythm of my heartbeat increased as I heard, "Coming to the stage, DAriya Larry."

It was July of 2022, and I was at an Alabama state pageant. It was actually held in Baton Rouge, Louisiana, and I was a contestant in the National American Miss Alabama pageant.

I knew I would go out there and do my best. I had already prepared, practiced, and prayed about my performance and even received uplifting words from the other girls, so I was ready. At that very moment, I mentally encouraged myself by saying my positive affirmations: I AM AMAZING. I AM CONFIDENT. I AM UNSTOPPABLE. I CAN DO ALL THINGS THROUGH CHRIST WHO STRENGTHENS ME.

What I wanted most was to go out there and do everything I had spent time working on so hard. I also wanted to make sure I connect with each judge in front of me, remember every word, make every step, and have fun in the process. I've competed in pageants before, with my first being in 2020, so I knew what to expect when it came to being on stage. My goal was to have a successful pageant experience, use my strengths to empower others, and make new friends while doing it, even during my nervous moments.

Right before I got ready to hit the stage, I could not stop my mind from racing and thinking about the past few months of my life. Having a brain injury and needing an emergency surgery became a big part of my life, and often reminded me of my struggles. I started to ask myself, "What if I trip, or worst, I fall during Formal Wear since my balance isn't 100%?" Before every performance, there was a question that had me so nervous. What if I forget my Personal Introduction speech? With my memory not being the same as before and having trouble retaining information, I ended up replacing that thought by saying, "You have your speech down packed."

Then came the interview. Wait, what if I say something weird or wrong? I had to regain my ability to speak not too long ago and was still working with a speech therapist on pronouncing my words correctly. My eyes grew big as I stood there worrying, but I tried to brush it off with a smile! All I could think about at first was all that could go wrong in those moments, but one of the most important things I did was change my negative thoughts to positive ones. I quickly reminded myself, "YOU ARE CAPABLE OF DOING ANYTHING YOU PUT YOUR MIND INTO. YOU ARE STRONG! YOU ARE BRAVE!"

Doing the pageant that weekend was what I wanted to do. This was what I chose to do because pageants are what I love to do, and I always have a good time while doing it. So what seemed like a long time thinking to myself actually ended up being just a short pause, a few deep breaths, and a couple of steps to center stage. It was time for me to get out there. DAriya, YOU GOT THIS!

Now don't get me wrong. Competing in pageant is fun. It offers many opportunities for girls to show off their talents, build confidence, develop public speaking skills, help focus on making a difference in their community, open doors to future connections, meet girls with the same mindset, and more. But it also comes with hard work and challenges. These challenges can impact your mental health in a negative way and could cause low self-esteem if you begin to look at what you don't have, focusing on someone else's beauty and outfits or how your walk doesn't look like the next person. But I'm here to tell you that what you have and how you look is more than enough. Maya Angelou once said, "Nothing can dim the light which shines from within."

As I was performing on stage, I gave it my all and let my light shine. Formal Wear done, Personal Introduction done, and interview done. I wasn't as nervous at all once I got to doing it because I knew I did my very best, and these were the moments I prepared for. Instead of allowing my negative thoughts to control how I was feeling and my performance during that time, I took control. And honestly, that's what it is all about sometimes! Taking our thoughts and feelings to make sure we have a healthy mental status during our pageant life.

Now, did I stumble on my speech during Personal Introduction? Yes. Did I trip on my gown during Formal Wear? Yes. Did I allow it to break me? No. Because we are not perfect, and not every moment in pageantry is going to be perfect. Things happen, but it's about how we take it. I had already overcome so much since being hospitalized at Children's of Alabama for 33 days; I knew that I was truly unstoppable. I was so proud of myself and filled with joy when I saw the smiles on my family's faces.

The support and positive words from my family during pageant weekend means so much to me. It helps to put me in the best place, knowing that they are there cheering me on every step of the way. It also helps me to feel less stressful hearing those encouraging words from my family and friends because pageants are not as easy as people think they are. When I add the positive affirmations I hear from my family with the ones I say to myself, it really motivates me and touches my heart. I love hearing "YOU ARE AMAZING" from those who care the most.

Being in pageants is not only about accomplishing your goal of winning a crown and a sash. For me, it is about appreciating the experience and growing in confidence. There will be ups and downs, twists and turns because pageants can be like roller coasters, but in the end, it can be so rewarding having great positive affirmations to carry with you. Although it took two years before capturing my very first title as the 2023 USA National Miss Southern States Jr. Teen, I have learned that the journey is just as important as any title, award, and destination.

Remember, you can do anything you put your heart and mind into! Sometimes it just takes time, but never give up on your dreams.

I created my platform StrongEnough to inspire and encourage others to overcome adversity and to know that when things get tough, don't get defeated because you are more than enough. After my brain surgery, I had to find my inner strength to continue doing the things that I loved to do. I understood the importance of a positive mental health and I want to see others be at their best, that can be through the use of positive affirmations.

One way you can get started with writing your own positive affirmations is to ask the people closest to you to describe you in one word. That could be intelligent, powerful, and a world changer. Then you would add the words "I AM" in front of it to say, "I AM INTELLIGENT, I AM POWERFUL, and I AM A WORLD CHANGER."

I encourage you to take a moment to reflect and write down empowering affirmations that you can recite daily. These positive affirmations will serve as a powerful reminder of your unique strengths and beauty. Embrace them wholeheartedly, and let their words of confidence and self-belief propel you towards your greatness!

Overcoming Adversity Using Positive Affirmations

Personal Reflections

Road to the Crown with Trinity Bush

Chapter 6
THE MENTAL ROLLERCOASTER
JAYLA GEORGE

You don't have to be great to start,
but you have to start to be great.
~ Zig Ziglar

Mental health is an emotional rush, especially when it comes to pageantry. One moment you could be prepared and ready to go on stage confidently. The next minute your nerves could take over and once you get off the stage, you would think that you didn't do so great, especially when you don't win a title. You make yourself feel like a failure, as if all your practices with the coaches didn't play out in reality how you wished it would.

I know this is how some girls my age, and maybe even younger, may feel when competing in a pageant because even I once felt like this. But through encouragement from my pageant coaches, I learned that having fun and talking to all the other girls help ease your nerves, as well as using some of the communication skills you learn from pageants on your everyday basis. It even helps you talk to new people.

Think about it! What am I doing? How am I going to remember all of this? Do I have all of the outfits I need? Will I be able to walk in my heels?

Okay, it's showtime. Hair, makeup, dresses. All done. I make sure I have everything backstage: my mom, coaches, other girls, attitudes. Butterflies in my stomach. I'm trying to make everyone happy, but what about me? Now I'm seeing girls melting down while their moms are yelling at them. Practicing and practicing over and over, their coaches telling them you are not here to make friends; you are here to compete.

I'm feeling like I'm in another timeline. What is going on here? Ok, focus. You got this. And then I go onto the stage. But my nerves are taking over. How did I do? What will my coach say? What will my mom say? How do I feel?

This roller coaster ride must stop. We need to know our worth. We need to understand that this pageant does not define who we are, and we shouldn't be looking for validation from others. I am confident. I am brilliant. My affirmations must continue. It's okay to speak up if we feel down and not like ourselves.

Affirmations. These are the things that would run through my head when I'm preparing myself to go onto the stage. But before I learned affirmations, I used to get super nervous and forget either my walk or my speeches. However, this one time, I decided to not let my nerves get the best of me by zoning out the things going on around me and going over my speech over and over again until it was my turn.

As the backstage helpers signal that it is my turn, I prepare myself to forget bits and parts of my speech. But from the start to the end of my speech, I realize I didn't forget a single word and felt really good until crowning time when I see more and more people in my division get troupes for the same speech I gave. Then I heard my number and name being called. And guess what? I won 3rd place for my speech! In my mind, I say I really did it as I accepted my reward with a great feeling.

Now that I've seen the magic in using affirmations and believing in myself, find new ways to make sure you do the same on an everyday basis, like using sticky notes and writing affirmations on them and sticking it on your room door. Or the next time you go to a pageant, put them in your hotel room or even in a personalize notebook or journal for when you feel overwhelmed, and write what made you so overwhelmed, That way, when you start doubting yourself, all you have to do is look at your affirmations to remind yourself that you are capable of doing anything you put your mind into.

Personal Reflections

Chapter 7
THE PIECES THAT MAKE ME, ME
AKEELAH SANDERS

I'm not weird. I'm limited edition.
~ J.T. Geissinger

Brave, confident, comfortable with who I am, and limited edition! I am Akeelah Sanders, a rising 8th grader who loves reading, writing, art, singing, modeling, and pageants. I've been competing in pageants since I was 9 years old. I watched my older sister compete for several years before beginning the journey myself.

Pageants have changed my life! I have been able to find my voice, advocate for causes important to me, make life-long friends, meet new people, encounter opportunities that I may not have been afforded otherwise, and overcome some of the things that have happened to me in my short life. And those are just a few of the benefits that I've experienced.

Like everything in life, there are some not so glamorous aspects of pageants and competitions. Pageantry is a sport, so there's this intense pressure to perform and excel, and an even greater pressure to be perfect because you are a role model and pillar in the community. Being so well-known can make girls feel paranoid about making mistakes.

The reality is that there can only be one winner, and as pageant girls, we hear no more than yes. Hearing no can make a person feel as if they aren't enough. A suggestion for preparing to hear more no's than yes's is to identify other goals to soften the impact hearing no can have on your mental health. So, I have several tips that I want to share with readers about the importance of mental health, self-care, and coping skills. And I'd like to begin by sharing my story before pageantry.

"Once upon a time…"

Every day I choose to put on a smile, but I did not have a traditional upbringing. I was placed in foster care system at the age of four. I moved around from foster home to foster home and experienced racism by my own biological family as well as in the system.

For a long time, I was bullied because I was awkward. When I'm asked questions, I would not always respond right away. I wasn't comfortable speaking up and using my voice, so I would make animal sounds or just choose to be non-responsive. Upon entering the foster care system, I was separated from my biological brothers. It was a situation where I could not see them regularly because it was unhealthy. I was placed in a different foster home where I thought I was being adopted. After settling into that home, I found out that the couple decided not to adopt me because I didn't look like them. I felt so sad and alone. I didn't feel like I was enough, and I didn't believe that I would ever find the support or help that I needed.

School wasn't much better. I was being bullied for being different. Kids made fun of my curly hair. I did not have any friends. I was alone, angry, hurt, defeated, and MAD. I started misbehaving at home and school. Luckily, a better situation was right around the corner.

"Sometimes things fall apart so that better things can fall together." - Marilyn Monroe

I was six when I met my forever family. I finally felt that I was where I belong. Despite my behavior, they accepted me. They showed me kindness and love right when I was starting to not love myself. The more I was around them, the more at home I felt. As I met my extended family, I knew this was where I wanted to be.

Shortly after moving in, I was diagnosed with anxiety and a processing delay. This diagnosis allowed me to get more help at school, and it allowed me to understand why I could not always find the words to respond to questions. I started competing in pageants to help me come out of my shell and grow my self-confidence. It was important for me to tell you about my past because it set the stage for shaping my pageant and mental health journey.

Ready... Set... Pageants!

Pageantry has become my primary hobby, and I love every moment of it even though there were times I felt that it did not love me. I joined pageants because I wanted to be confident when speaking to others, and I hoped that it would help with my long pauses and speech delays.

I competed for four years before I won my first state title. That was a total of nine No's before I heard a Yes. It's hard to want to keep trying after working so hard and feeling like you have failed. I started making jokes about being put in the Guinness Book of World Records for losing the most pageants in a row. I tried to use humor to cover up the sadness that losing repeatedly caused me. Combined with the feelings that I already had from my foster care experience, it would be easy to see how I could start feeling like I wasn't enough.

Another thing that can be hard about pageants is the pressure of winning. We watch our families sacrifice to provide us with these opportunities. More than just disappointing myself, losing sometimes felt like disappointing my biggest supporters. My family does not pressure me by saying that I have to win, but I'd be lying if I said I didn't feel pressured to win because I want to make them proud.

Lastly, the pressure of being perfect can be a lot to handle, especially for a teenager/young adult trying to figure out how to navigate life. When you put on a crown and a sash, you represent an entire organization. Your actions always have consequences, but those consequences seem greater when you are the face of an organization. The things that you do, the ways that you behave, can impact everyone involved. Perfection can mean different things to different people. I know girls who were scared to be judged for who they love, saying the wrong thing, and honest mistakes that were made as part of growing up.

Additionally, pageants ask us to speak our mind, but that's scary when everybody gets offended by different opinions. It's hard to be your complete self, and pretending to be who an organization wants you to be instead of who you are can impact young girls mentally.

Perfection can also be about having the right body type. If you're too large, you're unhealthy and may not be considered pretty enough or fit enough. If you are too small, it may play into the stereotypes of what everyone thinks of pageant girls. These thoughts lead to insecurities about how girls look, and they can have a negative impact on mental health. These may not be true statements about how organizations truly feel, but it can be the pageant girl's perception. Perception is reality. And there are things that we can do to protect ourselves and our mental health.

"This hurts, so I need to be extra kind towards myself."

Mental health management is so important. I know that there can be negative thoughts about people that go to therapy or those who express that they are suffering from a mental health crisis, but we have to continue to advocate for mental health. The scariest thing about poor mental health is that it can make you feel like you are the only one struggling, and that makes it hard to open up because you may not want to be judged. It's important to be kind to yourself, talk to someone that you can trust if you don't feel okay, and always remember that it's okay not to be okay.

It's also important to take time to process your feelings and feel whatever you feel. Surround yourself with people and things that you love. During my time in the different foster homes and when I was trying to make friends, I would try hard to get other people to like me. I spent so much time focused on who didn't like or love me that I almost missed out on a lot of good things and almost forgot that there were already people who love me for being me. Having a positive mindset can really help you be successful. Practice self-care and self-love, and have coping skills readily available.

Self-care and coping skills are important not just in pageants, but also in your life journey. Self-care is taking control of your mental health by doing things that make you feel good. It is something you do before you can have negative feelings. Meanwhile, coping skills are activities or things that you can do to help yourself deal with stressful situations. They are how you respond to negative things that happen to you, so it's like having a plan in place for when you need it.

My top three things to do as part of my self-care routine are:

> Goal setting; The reality is, everyone can't win. So I set goals that don't include winning like improving in an interview, genuinely feeling good and staying in good spirits about the week, meeting new people or doing one thing outside of my comfort zone throughout the pageant week. I also create vision boards that list my goals. It's good to have a reminder of the things that are important so that I don't get distracted.

> Stay connected and focus on gratitude; My family is such a source of support. My Dad always makes me laugh; he's silly and breaks tension and stress. And my Mom makes sure I eat and sleep properly, write me nice letters, get me gifts, encourage me, and hype me up with a dance party. My brother also makes jokes and talk a lot. My forever family has always helped and supported me through

pageants, everyday life, and even through my toughest moments. I know they will always be there for me, and I'm so thankful that I have them by my side. My pageant coaches, extended family, mentors, and friends encourage me as well. And I make it a point to stay connected to them and remind myself of how lucky I am to have them.

Help others; Helping other people makes me feel really good about myself. When I started my pageant journey, I created my personal platform which is #KindLikeKeelah. This platform was inspired by my forever family because before they knew me, they were kind to me. They took me in and completely changed my life. #KindLikeKeelah is all about recognizing the impact of being kind. You never know what people are going through, but with one smile or kind gesture, we have the power to change someone's day. I encourage people to spread kindness through volunteerism and just being mindful of how we can make someone's day better.

My self-care routine also involves watching a scary movie with my mom, listening to my dad's horrible dad jokes or trying new foods with him, listening to music and singing, burning candles, watching videos on YouTube, wrestling with my brother, and riding my bike around the neighborhood. It could also be taking a long shower and singing my favorite songs at the top of my lungs (even when it annoys my family lol). I make it a point that no matter how busy things get, I do at least one of these things each day. Self-care helps me feel refreshed, and it makes my heart happy. Find those things that bring you joy, and make time to do them!

Meanwhile, my top three things to do as coping skills when I am stressed are:

> Drawing; When my feelings feel too big for what I can handle and I can't talk about them, I draw out my feelings. I give myself permission to draw whatever I need to so that I can get the emotion out.

> Communicating; I am still working on being completely open about what I feel. My family is understanding and gives me time to process and express myself. I know it's hard to know when to give space and when to push, but be patient with yourself and your family while you figure it out. Please just don't stop communicating and allow yourself to feel alone.

> Taking a break; Sometimes the best thing to do is to take a temporary break from what's causing stress, anxiety or sadness. Go for a walk, meditate or pray.

Sometimes I even pull things from my self-care list to use as coping skills. It's important to have both self-care and coping skills. Think of self-care as building up your resilience or filling up your tank for when you need extra encouragement later. This helps you make sure you can handle situations that cause stress and/or anxiety. When those situations happen, coping skills are what you use to decompress. Coping skills are the way you let go of your emotions when you feel them.

"If you look for perfection, you'll never be content." - Leo Tolstoy

Nobody is perfect; perfection should not be expected. Trying to achieve it can make you feel very lonely and sad. It makes you isolate yourself from the people who love and care about you. I started this chapter with the quote, "I'm not weird. I'm limited edition," because it's giving me the confidence to just be me... unapologetically. Through the years, I have met a lot of new people and made a lot of new friends. I feel really good about how I've been able to grow. But this would not have been possible if I didn't practice mental health management.

I've shared a lot about what I've experienced in life and how I dealt with my own trauma. I wanted to be honest about my past because I know that everyone is going through their own struggles. When you look at me, you would never know that this is my story. You'd just see a happy teenager. I hope that sharing my story gives you courage to share yours, and that sharing your story helps you deal with any trauma you've experienced. Dealing with your emotions will positively impact your mental health.

The Pieces That Make Me, Me

Personal Reflections

Road to the Crown with Trinity Bush

Chapter 8
BREAKING THE STIGMA
KENNEDY FREENEY

*It's okay to not be okay;
it's not okay to stay that way.*
~ Unknown

Pageantry is a realm that's known for its glamour, glitz, and beauty. It provides a platform for women to exhibit their abilities, intellect, and resilience. There are numerous reasons for participating in pageants, including improving our self-confidence, honing our public speaking skills, advocating for a cause or platform, and having the chance to earn scholarships and/or rewards.

When I attended my first open call, I was only five years old and had no idea what I was signing up for. All I cared about was having fun and wearing a pretty dress (in my case, dressing up as Elsa) and looking like a princess. As I grew older, fear began to take a hold of me, but I refused to let it control me. Today, I am proud to be Kennedy Simone Freeney, your 2023 Miss Texas Jr. High United States. As a titleholder, I have the opportunity to make a positive impact to my community and inspire others to pursue their passions and goals.

Although pageantry is a competitive sport that involves beauty, grace, and poise, there are several stereotypes we face daily. For one, beauty queens are unintelligent and have no substance beyond their looks. Pageant girls are also often perceived as being overly concerned with their appearances and obsessed with their looks.

Pageantry can have a significant impact on the mental health of the contestants by imposing the pressure to attain perfection. During my time as a Lone Star Princess, I recall attending a workshop where I overheard one of the Miss Texas contestants being advised that she must always maintain a Miss Texas appearance. This advice revealed the level of pressure and expectations that contestants face, a dark side that often goes unnoticed. They are expected to have a flawless physical appearance, maintain a certain weight, and keep their hair and makeup perfect. Thus, the strain of attaining physical perfection can result in mental health issues.

As someone who has been participating in pageants since the age of 4, I know all too well how nerve-racking it can be to step onto the stage or into the interview room. The constant pressure to be perfect and deliver flawless responses can be overwhelming. I still vividly recall the time when I forgot my lines while saying my personal introduction on the national stage. It was an embarrassing moment, and I could have easily given up on pageantry altogether. However, the support and love from my fellow sister queens helped me to realize that it was okay to make a mistake and not to be perfect. Failure is a part of the learning process, and it is crucial to get back up and keep moving forward.

To compete at our best and truly enjoy the pageant experience, it is important to prioritize our mind. This is why I've learned that self-care is an essential aspect of maintaining a good mental health in pageantry. Here are a few self-care suggestions that I believe all contestants should keep in mind:

> Practice mindfulness; Living in the present moment without judgment through mindfulness can help you manage overwhelming or anxious feelings. Simply taking a few deep breaths and focusing on your breathing can make a difference.
>
> Take breaks; It's important to step away from the constant pressure of pageantry and recharge. You can do this by taking short walks, listening to music, meditating, or even dancing. Taking breaks can help you refocus and regain the energy you need to perform at your best.

Connect with loved ones; Family and friends provide a support system when things get tough. Reaching out to loved ones can help alleviate feelings of loneliness and isolation.

Set realistic goals; Setting realistic goals can help reduce the risk of disappointment and anxiety. Aim for achievable goals that will challenge you but won't cause unnecessary stress.

Prioritize sleep; It is crucial to get enough sleep to maintain good physical and mental health, especially in the world of pageantry. Proper sleep can significantly enhance your performance and help you tackle the challenges of pageantry with ease.

As participants in pageants, we possess an exceptional opportunity to champion mental well-being and promote understanding. Given our substantial viewership and influential status as role models, we can effectively raise awareness to effect positive change. Here are a few strategies to create an impact:

Utilize your platform; As pageant girls, we have an opportunity to reach a wide audience. We can leverage our social media platform and public appearances to bring attention to mental health issues and encourage others the importance of seeking help.

Share your story; Being transparent is a good thing because it prevents us from keeping our feelings and emotions bottled up inside. Therefore, sharing our own experiences can help break down the stigma and encourage others to seek help.

Help raise funds for mental health organizations; By organizing a fundraiser or hosting a charity event, you can support organizations that provide mental health services or advocacy.

Collaborate with your pageant organization; Work with the pageant organization you are currently representing to host a mental health workshop or event that brings awareness during pageant week, where you can share stress management techniques, mindfulness practices, and/or self-care strategies.

Mental health is a critical issue that affects millions of people worldwide. Unfortunately, there is still a significant amount of stigma surrounding mental illness, and many people do not seek the help they need due to the fear of being judged or discriminated against. It's important to recognize that mental health is just as vital as physical health, and it's crucial to encourage open and honest conversations about mental health to create a healthier society.

The first step to overcoming mental health problems is to seek help from a qualified professional, such as a therapist or psychiatrist. They can provide you with the necessary tools and support to manage your symptoms.

It's common to struggle with mental health. But seeking help is a sign of strength, not weakness, and it should not be ignored. To perform at your best, we need to maintain our mental health by implementing the proper practices.

Continue to radiate your brilliance and never let anyone make you feel inadequate.

Breaking the Stigma

Personal Reflections

Road to the Crown with Trinity Bush

Chapter 9
THREE HELPING HANDS
LONDYN VARNADO

Have you ever had to do tryouts? Maybe for sports, an orchestra, band, choir, theater, or even a pageant? Well, let me tell you about my incredible journey during my first and only pageant experience. It happened back in 2017 when I participated in the Little Miss Texas Unique International Preteen pageant. And guess what? I won the title! It was such an amazing moment that I will never forget.

But let me be honest with you. When I first stepped onto that stage, I was really nervous. My heart was racing, and I had butterflies in my stomach. It was scary, but you know what? It turned out to be so much fun! That pageant experience taught me something important about myself. It showed me that I am strong and capable of overcoming challenges. Winning that title made me feel powerful and empowered to take on even more exciting opportunities.

Hey, let me introduce myself. I'm Londyn Varnado, a girl who loves art, dancing, music, dogs, and watching movies. I'm still exploring what I want to be when I grow up. Maybe a dancer, actress or model. Who knows? I have time to figure it out. But one thing I know for sure is that tryouts are not easy. They can be stressful and make you lose confidence. That's why I'm here to share some ways to overcome those struggles.

When I entered high school, I decided to join the orchestra and the drill team. If you don't know what the drill team is, it's like my school's dance team. We perform at basketball and football games, competitions, and prep rallies. It's so much fun, but to make it on the team, you have to pass an audition.

I was nervous to try out for the drill team because I had never experienced a school tryout before. But I really wanted to be on the team, so I gave it a shot. My mom and I attended all the meetings and completed the paperwork. We were ready!

The tryouts finally arrived, and boy, was I tense! I was even more nervous than the word nervous can explain. But our dance director explained how the tryouts worked, and that helped calm my nerves a bit. We had four days of tryouts, where we learned the dance routine and kick routines. Then came the mock tryout day, where we practiced without judges, just to get a feel for the real thing.

But here's the twist! On the actual tryout day, there was a big storm with thunder and lightning. Can you believe it? So they had to postpone the tryouts to the next day. It gave me more time to practice the dance and go over every move. When the day finally came, I felt much better. I was prepared and equipped, which relieved me of stress and worry.

The day flew by, and before I knew it, I had only one hour to get ready for tryouts. I saw all the other girls, and guess what? They were just as nervous as I was! But you know what made the difference? We practiced together in the locker room, cracking jokes, and making each other laugh. We shared our worries and helped each other fix any mistakes. The stress simply vanished from the room.

Minutes before we started the tryouts, I found a quiet corner in the locker room. I knelt down on the cold concrete floor and prayed. I asked God to bless my feet, help me remember the dance, and keep all the girls from making mistakes. I also prayed for the judges to be kind. Then it was time to show what I've got!

As my group and I walked onto the gym floor, we took deep breaths and whispered words of encouragement to each other. We were ready to dance our hearts out. And that's exactly what we did. One, two, three, four, five, six, seven, eight... The dance steps flowed through my mind like a broken record, and I gave it my all.

Before I knew it, the tryouts were over. I felt great about how everything went, and I wished good luck to the girls who went after me. Then I sat down, thinking about the dance and imagining what the results would look like.

About 30 minutes later, I received an email from the dance director. I anxiously opened it and scrolled through the message. There it was – my audition number. I had made it onto the team! I couldn't contain my joy and excitement. I immediately shared the news with my dad, who was just as thrilled for me.

That feeling of accomplishment was incredible. Looking back on the tryouts, I realized that three things helped me stay calm and focused: practice, friends, and prayer. Practicing the dance over and over again made me feel confident and prepared. Being surrounded by supportive friends who shared the same nerves made the whole experience more enjoyable. And prayer, knowing that God was on my side, lifted all the worries off my shoulders.

These three things can help you conquer your own tryouts and keep your mental health stable. Practice, gather friends who lift you up, and seek guidance through prayer. Trust me, they make a world of difference.

Now, it's time for you to shine! Whatever tryouts you have in your future, remember that you have the strength and ability to overcome any challenge. Believe in yourself, stay positive, and never give up. With a little practice, the support of friends, and faith in yourself, you can achieve great things.

Well, that's it for now. I'm going to enjoy some TV time. Have an amazing day, and remember to chase your dreams with all your heart. Bye!

Three Helping Hands

Personal Reflections

Road to the Crown with Trinity Bush

Chapter 10
THE NATIONAL AMERICAN MISS TEEN
KAYLA TOURE

Jesus looked at them and said,
With man this is impossible,
but with God all things are possible.
~ Matthew 19:26

Who would have thought that a girl from an impoverished neighbor that subsisted on free drinks from the local soup kitchen would grow up to shine and add glitter to the glitzy and glamorous pageantry world? As a little girl, it was just a dream for me to wear a dress fit for a princess, but I never expected to wear a gown meant for a queen—and bag a crown at that! My journey in pageantry was long and arduous, as my life was filled with several trials and tribulations. However, despite the challenges, I still found the strength and motivation to achieve my goal.

My Humble Beginnings

Living in the projects made me witness the real-life drama and action that inspire blockbuster ghetto movies. All day and night, I would see people fighting, exchanging drugs, and hear police sirens break out gang brawls and arrest young perpetrators of crime. I see parents craning their necks, anxiously watching their children from the porch or through the windows because they are aware of the possibility of something terrible happening to them. However, this was the only place they could afford to raise them.

All around me, people were toughened by their negativity. They spoke of death, incarceration, their hopelessness at being homeless, and they tried to influence me by telling me that my life was doomed because of the environment I grew up in. Deep inside, I kept saying no to them because I chose to keep a positive mindset. I chose to see the blessing of having a roof over our heads and food to eat donated by people with compassionate hearts. I learned that I was an overcomer and that I would prevail. I also learned a massive lesson about homelessness and how the community serves homeless people, which made me pay attention to the good in people. Soup may not have been much to people who had many food choices, but soup was everything for my family and me because that was all we had to eat. Still, I knew we deserved better. In this poverty, my struggles motivated me to seek a better life for myself and my family.

My Journey to the Crown

As I became an adult, I started looking into colleges and jobs I could work that would put me in a better situation than when I was growing up. By a stroke of luck, I was able to enter the world of pageantry. I willingly jumped in with a fairy tale-like vision of constant happiness and fame as I rubbed elbows with the rich and famous. I would travel a lot and enjoy a life of luxury, and all the while, enjoy the attention and admiration of everyone. Fortunately, I did bag the crown and became a beauty queen. My dream of confidently walking across the stage with a beaming smile that could light up a room and a sparkling tiara atop my head eventually came true! But little did I know that pageantry was beyond the shine and shimmer because it presented avenues for engagement with various organizations and the ability to impact lives positively.

My Venous Malformation Story

While some people give in to societal tremendous pressures, in my case, my stress and anxiety manifested into physical symptoms. It was in the year 2020. I remember the day like yesterday. I had not planned on visiting urgent care. During the trip, I could feel intense anxiety because I somehow developed a massive lump on the side of my face. That single visit to urgent care was just like a regular check-up at the doctor's office. The doctor told me to use a warm rag for the swelling and prescribed me some medication.

A week passed, but the lump on my face was not subsiding. Nothing I did helped. I began to fear what this lump could be and started having an upset stomach as I looked in the mirror. The doctor told me, "If it does not go away this time, then you should probably go to the emergency room or see your pediatric doctor." A single visit to the ENT changed my life forever. After going to the hospital and Pediatrics, they still did not know my diagnosis, and I felt helpless. I could no longer control my emotions, and nothing made me happy.

After three long weeks, The MRI at the ENT finally revealed my Arteriovenous Malformation (AMV) diagnosis. All I could hear was the doctor saying that I would die from this medical diagnosis and that there was only a 1% cure for this disease; I felt like my heart was falling out of my chest. I remember this event so vividly because of the intense emotions inside me. I suddenly lost all confidence, and my passion for being in pageants was struck down.

Although I had many unanswered questions, I only saw a strong, brave girl who was forced to show vulnerability for a while. The way I dressed had not changed, nor did my personality. However, when I returned to school after the pandemic hit, everyone made fun of me like I was not the pretty girl I always was—this moment had me shaking like a leaf because I thought about how I would make it through life with this lump on my face. As I went on day by day working on my confidence with AMV, I realized other essential things about pageantry. I opened my eyes to the fact that pageantry is not all about looking good on the outside. It is being confident in who you are. Pageantry is about having a beautiful soul on the inside and out. Even though this diagnosis took a toll on my confidence at first, it made me realize that life comes with things we cannot change, but these things make us unique.

My saga with illness did not end there. A year later, after my diagnosis with AMV, I was diagnosed with hair loss, also known as Alopecia, where a person unexpectedly loses their hair in patches. My mother and I were both distressed about my hair. We had to have our hair nice and wear certain styles to compliment outfits on almost all the pageants. I lost my reputation as "Kayla with the big fro". It was a brutal realization because I had just learned how to accept my diagnosis with AMV. Both diagnoses were life-changing, but these taught me about the pageant industry and my appearance. Although people in school made jokes about me, I knew I had to stand up, love myself, and be confident without my hair, just like I was when I still had it. With that, my self-esteem was boosted.

Pageantry's Impact on Mental Health

As a pageant queen, I know the intense pressure to meet societal beauty standards can affect one's mental well-being. Pageantry can be highly demanding and competitive, with contestants often facing tremendous responsibilities and stress. The pressure to maintain a poised demeanor, present flawlessly, and look perfect can be overwhelming. One may face comparisons, judgment, and criticism, negatively impacting confidence and self-esteem. Similarly, the pageant preparation's rigorous media commitments, appearances, rehearsals, and schedule can lead to mental fatigue, burnout, and exhaustion.

The stress and responsibilities multiply as a national titleholder since audiences expect much from the queen. I stepped into multiple roles, such as being a role model, advocate, and spokesperson. I had to fulfill various obligations, attend events, manage public appearances, and travel extensively while maintaining a positive public image and balancing personal commitments. This constant demand to meet expectations and perform resulted in immense stress and pressure, which affected my mental health.

My Advice to Pageant Queens

So, my dear pageant queens, here is some advice for you. It is beneficial to ensure you don't stress yourself and prioritize your mental health over competing. If you find yourself struggling with your mental health, try doing the following:

- ❖ Managing your expectations by remembering that it is normal to make mistakes and that perfection is not attainable. Thus, it is essential to recognize your expectations for yourself and others and practice self-acceptance and self-compassion. My own AMV and Alopecia are default flaws that I have embraced, and I know these can hinder me from achieving some goals. However, I still need to try.

- ❖ Set your boundaries and manage your commitments effectively. Prioritizing self-care over excessive obligations and learning to say no when needed is essential. Hence, it would be best to remember that setting limits and taking breaks is necessary. As a young titleholder, I thought I was unstoppable until my body could not take it anymore. So, take time to breathe and rest, my dear ladies!

- ❖ Practice self-care through self-nurturing, stress reduction, and relaxation activities. These include journaling, meditating, and exercising. These helped me enormously.

- ❖ Seek support from mental health professionals, friends, and trusted family members for assistance and guidance. Also, it would be best if you acknowledged that it is okay to prioritize your well-being and ask for help. You are human first before a pageant queen!

Pageantry can have both significant positive and negative impact on mental health. The responsibilities and stress accompanying a national pageant titleholder can affect your mental well-being due to the pressure to compete, meet expectations, and perform constantly. These can increase anxiety, stress, and depression.

Thus, it is important for you pageant queens to manage the impact of pageantry on your well-being and prioritize your mental health. I have been there myself, and my advice to you, my dear pageant queens, is to take it easy. Enjoy your moment and surround yourselves with a support system, including mental health professionals, family, and friends. At the slightest hint of mental health pressures, stop and start caring for yourself with the tips I shared.

Being a pageant queen may be a dream come true for you, but make sure that it is not the dream that will break you, making you unable to live it out as an inspiration to others. Just look at me and my journey to the crown. It was riddled with a whole spectrum of challenges! However, my faith, determination, and positive mindset got me through it all. I wish the same for you.

The National American Miss Teen

Personal Reflections

Road to the Crown with Trinity Bush

MEET THE AUTHORS

TRINITY BUSH
BEYOND WHAT YOU SEE

www.BeyondWhatYouSee.net

IG: TrinityBush15

FB: TrinityBush15

Captivating, empowering, and strong. Trinity Bush is the 12-year-old powerhouse hailing from Charlotte, North Carolina.

Ever since Trinity was able to speak, she has been tantalizing and captivating the attention of those around her. Her larger-than-life personality and spunkiness are beautifully displayed each time she takes the pageant stage. Trinity holds many pageant titles, and she is most proud of her 2019 North Carolina National American Miss Jr. Preteen, 2021 North Carolina Global Continental Preteen, and 2022 National Global Continental Preteen titles.

As a busy 7th grader at Southlake Christian Academy, Trinity is a girl who loves to discover new things. She loves science, American sign language, basketball writing, and reading!

Trinity is the true definition of well-roundedness. Not only is she a pageant queen, but she is also a skilled dancer, academically successful student, and money-making CEO. She is a 3-time Amazon Best Seller, A/B Honor Roll student, recipient of the 2020 S.T.R.E.A.M New Entrepreneur Award, and the visionary author of a powerful anthology series titled "The Road to the Crown".

Interviewing with adult judges, giving personal introduction speeches from the stage, and delivering inspiring monologues, she leaves it all on the stage over and over, only sometimes taking the medal crown, but always taking the crown of self-confidence and picking herself up from failures and turning them into life lessons. She began helping her peers build their self-esteem and encouraging others to embrace their perfect imperfections with her original monologue "Too Tiny". Trinity truly wants every child to win!

Meet the Authors

Her passion for helping others grew, and she turned her platform into a business. Trinity is the founder and CEO of Beyond What You See, LLC. Its mission is to empower and inspire kids and adults alike to embrace their perfect imperfections, feel their fears yet do what they love anyway, and to look beyond what they see in the mirror to find their true inner strength. She accomplishes that mission through keynote speaking, being a dynamic author, affirmation slanger, and through an affirmation clothing line. She is also the bestselling author of "The Science Behind It" (2020), "The Road to The Crown" (2021), and "The Road to The Crown Vol. II" (2022).

Confidence doesn't come when you have all of the answers, but it comes when you are ready to face all of the questions, and Trinity is facing them all head-on.

TRINITY WOULD LIKE TO ACKNOWLEDGE.

Patrice Bush (mom), Maurice Bush (dad), Kylah Thompson, Jurnee Bush, James Webb, Patricia Jackson, Deleisha Webb, Cedric Blackwell, Donna Murrell, Ardulla Gutherie, Emily Cox

SELENE M.K FERDINAND
MEERA EMPOWERMENT INC.

Meeraempowerment.org

@seleneFerdinand

Selene M.K Ferdinand is a 10-year-old girl hailing from New York. In addition to attending Dutch Broadway Elementary School, she wears many hats in her "spare" time. She is the CEO of Meera Empowerment INC, co-host for You're Our Unity on Strong Island Television Station, co- author of Road to the Crown Vol 2, Girl Scout of Nassau County, dancer, actress, model, designer, singer, and chef. Six years ago, Selene joined the NAM sisterhood, winning several titles throughout the years, and shares what NAM has done for her friends, family and most importantly her community. NAM has shown her that if she fails to prepare then she is prepared to fail. NAM has given her confidence on the stage and off the stage when the lights are off. NAM has challenged her to put words into action through numerous hours of community service.

It's no secret that serving your community, no matter how big or small, will provide long lasting effects for others—whether it's donating toys, clothing, and books to children in need, supporting organizations like Building Homes for Heroes, Ronald Mc Donald House, Island Harvest or volunteering at the Sun Harbor Manor Nursing Home providing a day of fun for the elderly.

This past year, Selene wanted to make her dream become her reality, which is why Meera Empowerment INC. was created. At Meera Empowerment, we believe that the best opportunities for personal growth come from hands-on experiences. This is the motivation behind our Community Service Program, where participants are encouraged to explore the world, enjoy all of life's moments, and give back to others. Meera Empowerment programs are developed to be inclusive of all backgrounds and skill sets in mind, providing the perfect platform to connect, learn, and grow.

In the upcoming year, the platform's goals include surpassing the amount of community service hours from our launch year, calling all hands on deck by all participants, and reducing the carbon footprint by focusing on reducing waste and recycling plastic cans and bottles, all while raising funds to donate to great causes like the American Cancer Society. In the future, Selene hopes to earn her white coat and contribute to the research for a world that is cancer-free. NAM has shown that without help in one form or another, hope can mean nothing, so let's continue to offer genuine service to others, not just hope, to see a better future.

SELENE WOULD LIKE TO ACKNOWLEDGE.

My Mom, Dad and Brother Stefan,
Meara Empowerment Team & Ambassador,
Elmont Strong Organization, Girl Scout Troop 1080,
The Hall Family, The Sahadeo Family, The Seegobin Family,
The Hansraj Family, The Lewis Family,
The Campbell Family, The Solages Family,
The Sanon Family, Debra Clark, Troy Alexander,
Leshawn Walker, Keyana Augustin, Dale Davids,
Desiree Nelson, Zhara Collins, Vernell Nelson,
Anniah Marajdeen, Monique Hardial, Anennte Deyer Smith,
Melzeta Fowler

DARIYA LARRY
STRONGENOUGH

IG- @dariya_marie

IG- @strongenough__

FB- DAriya Marie

Leaving a little sparkle everywhere she goes, DAriya Larry is a 12-year-old dream chaser from Birmingham, Alabama. Since beginning her journey in pageantry in 2020, DAriya has continued growing in confidence while spreading love through community service. She has been able to make a difference in the lives of others at Jessie's Place Women and Children Shelter, First Light Shelter, Children's of Alabama, the Community Food Bank of Central Alabama, and her newest project, the Ronald McDonald House Charities of Alabama. DAriya currently holds the title of the

2023 USA National Miss Southern States and enjoys making appearances and sharing all the great things about her title.

While striving to be the best for others in her community, DAriya works just as hard in the classroom as a rising 8th grader who loves learning with History and Math being her favorite subjects. She is multi-talented with skills in dancing, piano, and tumbling. Not only is she well-rounded, but she is a very strong girl whose mission has been to bring awareness to brain injuries and its effects on those impacted by it. After her brain surgery in 2022, DAriya founded her platform StrongEnough to remind others that they are resilient. She puts her passion of inspiring others to overcome adversities by sharing her handmade affirmation bracelets and more.

DAriya believes that not everyone has to wear a sparkling crown on their head to be a queen, but wearing it in your heart is just as great because it's what we do from the heart that counts the most.

DARIYA WOULD LIKE TO ACKNOWLEDGE.

RaShaun Larry, DAris Scarver, Skylar Scarver, Donna Scarver, Anthony Jennings, Kenneth & Laurtha Hopson, Lisa Germany, Monique Germany, Rakeya Morrow, Tikia Ellison, Patrick Larry, Emma Larry, Laquita Larry, Ryan Jones, Alysha Shaw, LaTorria & Junius Harris

JAZEL BELLA JOHNSON
J.BELLA

www.jazelbella.com

IG: @jazelbella FB

Twitter: Jazel Bella Johnson

She has a magic that is all her own. Her name is Jazel Bella Johnson.

Jazel Bella Johnson, affectionately known as J. Bella, is a 12-year-old pageant queen, model, dancer, community activist, and kid CEO. Her beautiful and charismatic personality has captured the hearts of people all over the world and has opened many doors of opportunity.

Jazel Bella participated in her first pageant in 2018. As a novice in the pageant world that year, she represented the great state of Pennsylvania and was crowned Miss Philadelphia Jr. Preteen, a title she held for two consecutive years. In 2022, she won Miss Pennsylvania Preteen Actress, Talent & Community Service Activist, and in 2019, Miss Pennsylvania Jr. Preteen Talent, Actress, Casual Modeling and Most Promising Model along with numerous other awards and accolades. She won National Ambassador for 2018-2109 and 2019-2020. She also won a Miss Personality Award at the National pageant.

Her charismatic and contagious personality is a sure contributor to her earning each of those crowns. Jazel Bella loves participating in pageants for many reasons, but most of all she enjoys meeting new friends and having the opportunity to connect with people from all around the world.

In addition to being a natural beauty, Jazel Bella is also a brilliant student. As a current 7th grader, she is a straight A honor roll student who speaks 3 languages and excels in language, arts, science, and math. She was selected and sworn into the Philadelphia Community Youth Court in 2022, where she plays an integral role in encouraging and leading her peers to be honorable students and individuals in life. She was awarded 'The Leader Award" this year in her 7th grade class for showing and leading the way for her peers and all she encounters. She also has a love for basketball and was awarded the MVP award for her middle school team and the "Empowerment Award" at HoopHers. Jazel Bella is a star student and athlete who loves supporting her classmates and always makes new students feel welcome with her warm and inclusive personality.

Not only is Jazel Bella a talented student, but she is also a kid CEO who is very active in her community. In 2017, Jazel Bella and her family launched the J. Bella brand and clothing company. Through her business, she hopes to inspire others, especially girls, to love themselves and embrace their unique style. As a young CEO, she uses her platform, J.Bella L.O.V.E.S., and resources to serve her community by volunteering at the local nursing home, local food bank, Rescue Mission homeless shelter, and her youth reading program.

In her spare time, Jazel Bella loves to play with her younger brother, participate in activities such as ballet, praise dancing, acrobatics, tap, hip-hop, tennis, basketball, chess club, and swimming. Jazel Bella has been featured as a guest on FOX 29's "Q Show". She also led the countdown and performed a dance solo at the District 9 Holiday Christmas Tree lighting.

In 2021, Jazel Bella became a #1 Amazon Best-Selling author. In her book titled "Road to the Crown", an anthology, she shares her story of perseverance and triumph in the world of pageantry. In her chapter, Jazel Bella reminds readers to strive for greatness and excellence in all things.

In 2022, she continued to flex her writing muscles as an author in "Road To The Crown Volume II", where she shares the importance of her business & how to lead the way as a young entrepreneur. She also became a two-time best-selling author.

In the future, Jazel Bella Johnson plans to be a world-famous designer and lawyer. Until then, her focus is on making the world a better place to live, love, and shine.

JAZEL WOULD LIKE TO ACKNOWLEDGE.

Jamar (Dad) & Dr. Louisa (Mom) Johnson & Jamar Jr.,
GrandPa Gaiter, Grammy Johnson,
GrandMa Sarah Blain Jones, GMAC Joyce, Uncle RaShawn,
Daymond Yasmeen, & Christian,
Auntie Regina & Jean Skeeters, Uncle Brenton,
The Blain Family, Cunningham Family, The Douglas Family,
The Gaiter Family, Hassell Family, Mills Family,
Hawkins Family, Aunties Yandy Smith-Harris, Latia, Tika,
Jeanelle, Chelsea', Jade JeJuan, &Tashyra Ayers, The Smith's,
Spain Family, Jesse DeBerry.
In Loving Memory of GrandMa Feena Blain Gaiter

ZARIA MARTIN RILEY
MORE THAN A MODEL

www.morethanamodel.org
IG: I_AM_MoreThan
FB:More Than a Model
Twitter: Imorethn

Zaria is a remarkable and devoted young woman who excels in academics, community service, and the world of pageantry. Despite her tender age of 11, she has already made a profound impact on her school and local community, utilizing her exceptional talents and passions to bring about positive transformations.

Zaria consistently demonstrates her unwavering commitment to academic excellence as one of the top-performing students at S. Christa McAuliffe Elementary School. With a special affinity for Writing and Health, she envisions a future as a mental health professional, driven by her desire to make a meaningful difference in the lives of others.

Beyond her academic pursuits, Zaria actively engages in community service, dedicating her time and energy to organizations like Manna and Project Give Back. Her volunteer work has nurtured a profound passion for empowering fellow youth in areas of self-esteem and public speaking, positioning her as a supportive role model at such a young age.

Zaria has also made a name for herself in the world of pageantry, leaving an indelible mark through her participation in prestigious events such as FTM Fashion Week and New York Fashion Week. Her success can be attributed to her unwavering confidence and relentless determination. Through pageantry, she has developed crucial life skills, including empathy and discipline, which she believes will propel her personal growth and future accomplishments.

In her leisure time, Zaria finds solace and expression in creating bracelets, modeling, and doing nails. These activities not only provide her with balance but also help her stay connected to her authentic self. Furthermore, she is a passionate advocate for

Meet the Authors

youth advocacy and actively participates in More Than a Model, an organization co-founded by her mother. Together, they strive to foster equitable opportunities and resources for underserved populations.

In summary, Zaria epitomizes compassion and determination, eagerly seeking to make a meaningful impact in her school, community, and beyond. Her peers draw inspiration from her, recognizing the immense potential of young individuals to effect positive change in the world.

ZARIA WOULD LIKE TO ACKNOWLEDGE.

Mommy & Daddy, Brianne "Bri" Anderson, D Weekes, Grandma Bubba, Aunt Marilyn, Aunt Marlene, Aunt Dedra, Ms. Ursula Ricks, Godmommy, Aunt Reana, Aunt Kiki, Grandpa Dennis, Goddaddy, Christina & Kayden, Ms. Tara Pickstock, Uncle Dennis, Mrs. Titania Bailey, Uncle Freddy, GrounD BreakerS Baseball Academy (G3BA), Mrs. Latoya Scott, Nurse Jade, Mrs. Wanda Coates

JAYLA ALANI GEORGE
T.E.A.M, LTD. CO

Confident, the FAITH in myself is unshakable; the affirmations she lives by! Jayla Alani George is a lively 13-year-old who was born in Houston, Texas, but also has a second home in Opelousas, Louisiana. Jayla loves riding horses, riding a tractor on the farmland, 4-wheeling, swimming, and spending time with her family and friends. She has always had a love for journaling and expressing herself, which have always been her strong points. She is presently in the 7th grade attending International Leadership of Texas-Katy, learning both mandarin and Spanish.

Jayla enjoys participating in many roles in school from student council to running track and maintaining an A/B honor roll. She also plans to pursue her dream of becoming a scientist, specifically a biochemist. Her nonprofit is T.E.A.M. Ltd, which collaborates with several other nonprofits to aid in the community by providing services to the elderly and hosting back-to-school drives. Jayla has held many titles, but is presently Miss Teen Louisiana, and plans to use her crown to continue T.E.A.M building awareness, as her motto is Together Everyone Achieves More.

JAYLA WOULD LIKE TO ACKNOWLEDGE.

Norma & Paul George III and the George Family,
Hubert Batiste Sr. & The Late Mary Sampy Batiste,
Eva Dell George & The Late Paul J George, Jr,
Uncle Reese (Hubert, Jr) and Nanny Karen Batiste,
Nanny Charlotte Johnson,
Nanny Yvette and Uncle Jason Bernard,
Justine Sampy- Tip-Tap- Toe Dance School, Meredith Kea,
Janne Cluse, Sherita Calais Thomas, Beverly Batiste,
Raquel Zenon, Demathus Ledet,
Sachet Lane (Pink Pearls Too),
Tamesha King, Melinda Sampy Green,
Lisa and Sylvester Trufant.

KENNEDY FREENEY
KENNEDY SIMONE

www.kennedysimone.com

IG:@_iamkennedysimone_

FB: iamkennedysimone

Kennedy is a 14-year-old honor student who is a shining example of what it means to be a driven, talented, and passionate young woman. A Dallas, Texas native, Kennedy has always been a devout Christian, and her faith has been a guiding force in her life. She loves attending church and participating in youth group activities, and she often uses her platform as a pageant queen to spread the message of God's love and kindness.

Kennedy is not only a dedicated student but also an accomplished dancer. She is a squad leader on her school's dance team and spends countless hours perfecting her routines and leading her team to success. But Kennedy's love of dance extends beyond her school team. She is a company dancer at Dream Dance Conservatory as well as an ambassador for Brown Girls Do Ballet, where she is passionate about breaking down barriers for young women of color in the world of dancing.

In addition to Kennedy's academic and dance pursuits, at the young age of 13, she published her first book, "Road to the Crown Vol. II", and is currently working on her second book, "Road to the Crown Vol. III", which is a collaboration of inspirational stories written by several other dynamic women. Kennedy hopes to continue to inspire others with her words.

Of course, it's not all work and no play for Kennedy. She loves spending time with her family and friends, and she enjoys going on adventures and exploring new places. No matter where she goes or what she does, Kennedy always keeps her faith at the forefront of her life, and she is grateful for every opportunity that comes her way.

Kennedy is an exceptional young woman who is sure to make a positive impact on the world and those around her. With her talent, dedication, and faith, she is a true inspiration to everyone who knows her.

KENNEDY WOULD LIKE TO ACKNOWLEDGE.

Kewanna Freeney (mom), Duante Freeney (dad), Nila & Craig Ricks, Vinecia Williams, Desean Robinson, Michella Young, Devonna Coleman, Shyla Kristine Stone.

LONDYN LEEANN VARNADO

https://londynlvarnado.com/

FB: LondynLVarnado

IG: LondynLVarnado

londynlvarnado@gmail.com

Londyn is a talented and driven young woman who has accomplished a great deal at just 15 years old. Born in Memphis, Tennessee, she quickly discovered her love of the arts and began pursuing them with passion and dedication.

Growing up, Londyn showed an early talent for music and began playing the violin at a young age. She quickly excelled in her studies and soon began performing in the orchestra at her school and in competitions. Her dedication to her craft paid off tremendously, and there's no doubt that she will continue to make waves in the world.

Music isn't the only talent that Londyn possessed. She also has a passion for modeling and pageantry and began competing in local pageants and runway shows. Her natural poise and confidence on stage makes her a natural fit for the modeling industry.

Despite her busy schedule, Londyn still finds the time to pursue other interests. She joined her school's drill team where she can showcase her dancing skills and athleticism. She also continues to practice her violin and participate in music competitions, earning accolades and recognition for her performances.

Throughout all her accomplishments, Londyn remains grounded in her faith. As a devout Christian, she sees her talents and accomplishments as gifts from God, and uses them to inspire and uplift others. Her dedication to her faith, combined with her hard work and talent, have made her an inspiration to others.

Now living in Dallas, Texas, Londyn continues to pursue her many talents and interests, adding another accomplishment to her already impressive list of achievements by becoming a published author of "Road to the Crown Vol. III". This latest accomplishment is a testament to Londyn's creativity and determination. Not content with simply excelling in one area, she has continued to explore her passions and find new ways to share her message with the world.

LONDYN VARNADO
WOULD LIKE TO ACKNOWLEDGE.

Mom, Dad, Mr. Charles, Paris Varnado,
Mary Varnado (Nana), Anitra Smith (Tete),
Kimberly Peoples (Ms. Kim), Mrs. Whitney Kriewaldt,
Ms. Kewanna Freeney, Rosalind Harrison, Ms. Chen,
Ms. Maya Hayes, The late Mr. Isacc Birdlong, Jesus Christ.

AKEELAH SANDERS

www.akeelahmckenzie.com

IG: @akeelah.mckenzie

FB: @AkeelahSanders

Brave, confident, comfortable in her skin, and limited edition! Akeelah Sanders is a rising 8th grader who loves art, singing, modeling, and pageants.

Akeelah recently discovered her love for writing while taking a Creative Writing elective course. She frequently writes short stories and shares them with her friends and family. And she hopes to combine her love for writing and art by creating her own set of animated short stories for publication.

Akeelah's platform is #KindLikeKeelah, inspired by her forever family because before they knew her, they were kind and accepted her for who she is. Her forever family took her in and completely changed her life.

#KindLikeKeelah is all about recognizing the impact of being kind. You never know what people are going through, and with one smile or kind gesture, we have the power to change someone's day. She encourages people to spread kindness through volunteerism and just being mindful of how we can make someone's day better. Only light can cast out darkness, and she spreads her light throughout her community, which led to her being a 2021 Ben's Bellee Honoree, 2022 Fab Kids Against Bullying Award recipient, and the 2023 Pacer's National Bullying Prevention Center's Unity Award recipient, all for her work in the community.

A force to be reckoned with on the runway, an avid volunteer in her community, and now adding published author to her accolades, Akeelah is taking each opportunity that's afforded to her and taking the world by storm.

Road to the Crown with Trinity Bush

AKEELAH WOULD LIKE TO ACKNOWLEDGE.

Tanesia L. Anderson, Chris and Lydia Baker,
Quintina Hardesty Becker, PhD, Adelaide Bennett,
Kassie Diaz, USMC Veteran, PhD Student,
Peterlaena Gyimah and the Gyimah Family,
Whitney and Emilia Hernandez and the Hernandez Family,
Makisha & Chloe Hiller, Jess Nolan, Joshua Sr.,
Joshua Jr. & Apache Sanders,
Rev. Dr. & Dr. Robert (Anita) Sanders, Charlotte Watkins,
Shayla Watkins, Brooklyn Wells,
Aubri White & Skai Johnson, Regan White,
Isaiah & Regina Swopes, Calisi & Kai Solei Williams,
Maroco and Candace Williams, Tony & Eva Williams

KAYLA TOURÉ

Kayla Touré is an 18-year-old with a bright future. Coming from a partially West African family, Kayla is determined to excel in education and her career. Although she faces challenges with a Venous Malformation condition, she has resolved not to give up. As a second-generation immigrant with the emotional and social isolation experience that comes with her condition, Kayla has enrolled as a first-year student to study and major in Acting for Film, Television, Voiceover, and Commercial at Pace University. Her drive for success and passion for the performing arts is her major opportunity to inspire the world.

Having a Venous Malformation condition has stirred her firm belief and passion for spreading hospitality. It has propelled her to create her international movement called Kindness With Kayla, which promotes kindness while advocating for those with similar or different disabilities. She has managed to overcome her condition, braced up with determination, and has earned prestigious titles such as the current 2022-2023 National American Miss Teen and 2022 National American Miss New York Teen. Her participation in pageantry has emboldened her with confidence and intelligence, grooming her into a great young leader of her generation.

Kayla looks forward to becoming a professional actress and harbors dreams of performing in movies, commercials, and on Broadway. She is effortlessly committed to her aim of receiving prestigious awards like Tony, Oscar, Emmy, Academy, and many more in the entertainment industry by attending classes to immerse knowledge of her career, learning the improvisation techniques that are so essential for any aspiring artist. Winning any of these awards will unlock more ambitious projects in her career.

She knows the importance of grasping a clear understanding of script analysis, which is the core for better performance in this industry, so she strives to be on par. Kayla also actively works a lot on networking with other like-minded professionals, helping her get audition roles that help her showcase her talent and giving her exposure to different styles and genres, which can help her expand and explore new opportunities. The network and auditions provide her with valuable experience even if she did not get to participate, hence building her professional portfolio. Kayla is honing her career with persistence and focus, thus transitioning into an accomplished ambassador due to her great love for writing and performing her work. She is so dedicated to pursuing her dreams despite the challenges.

Her willingness and readiness to work hard regardless of her physical challenge, polishing her craft, and employing the necessary effort and dedication, have remained the sole goal in her quest to build a brand for herself in the film industry. She believes that the possibility and inspiration to achieve her dreams are drawn from those who had previously traveled this path with similar challenges and successfully achieved their goals through hard work and determination, proving that anything is possible. She is a firm believer that her success as an actress of color with a physical challenge will be an example—an inspiration for others around her and beyond—passing a message that no matter your skin color, where you come from, or the obstacles you face on your way, your success are not determined by these external factors.

Kayla aims to be a living example to others, especially those from similar backgrounds, to give encouragement and let them know that no matter how bad your starting point in life is or was, you can still achieve great things with hard work, dedication, and confidence in your abilities.

KAYLA TOURE' WOULD LIKE TO ACKNOWLEDGE.

Latifah Burns Toure, Jamicke Burns,
Renee Zander, Monica Pierre Louis,
Jorge Esteban of Pageant Smart, Hakrou Toure

www.ingramcontent.com/pod-product-compliance
Lightning Source LLC
Chambersburg PA
CBHW071004080526
44587CB00015B/2348